Family and *Friends*

ADDRESS
BOOK

HEARST BOOKS
New York

Foreword

How many times have I felt the wave of panic that sweeps over me when I mislay my address book? In my frustration at having lost it, I find it ironic that I can recall the details of a day long past — such as the color of the sky the time that a friend and I took a Sunday drive in the country that, on a whim, ended up winding lazily through three states — yet I cannot even retain a phone number.

It is for this reason that the address book was created. It is an essential reference book that should have been on the table next to my phone the last time I lost it, but in its much-demanded use, tends to get misplaced. So I stopped my frenzied search knowing that it would eventually turn up. And it did. And do you want to know the first thing I did when I found it? I called up that friend and made arrangements for another Sunday drive.

RACHEL NEWMAN
EDITOR-IN-CHIEF
COUNTRY LIVING

ANIMALS ARE
SUCH AGREEABLE FRIENDS—
THEY ASK NO QUESTIONS,
THEY PASS NO CRITICISMS.

George Eliot

'WHAT IS THE USE OF A BOOK,' THOUGHT ALICE, 'WITHOUT PICTURES OR CONVERSATIONS?'

Lewis Carroll

A

NAME

ADDRESS

PHONE

FAX

NAME

ADDRESS

PHONE

FAX

NAME

ADDRESS

PHONE

FAX

NAME

ADDRESS

PHONE

FAX

NAME ....

ADDRESS ....

....

.... PHONE

.... FAX

....

NAME ....

ADDRESS ....

....

.... PHONE

.... FAX

....

NAME ....

ADDRESS ....

....

.... PHONE

.... FAX

....

NAME ....

ADDRESS ....

....

.... PHONE

.... FAX

NAME ....

ADDRESS ....

....

....PHONE

....FAX

NAME ....

ADDRESS ....

....

....PHONE

....FAX

NAME ....

ADDRESS ....

....

....PHONE

....FAX

NAME ....

ADDRESS ....

....

....PHONE

....FAX

B

Name

Address

Phone

Fax

Name

Address

Phone

Fax

Name

Address

Phone

Fax

Name

Address

Phone

Fax

NAME ....

ADDRESS ....

....

.... PHONE

.... FAX

NAME ....

ADDRESS ....

....

.... PHONE

.... FAX

NAME ....

ADDRESS ....

....

.... PHONE

.... FAX

NAME ....

ADDRESS ....

....

.... PHONE

.... FAX

NAME ....

ADDRESS ....

....

.... PHONE

.... FAX

....

NAME ....

ADDRESS ....

....

.... PHONE

.... FAX

NAME ....

ADDRESS ....

....

.... PHONE

.... FAX

NAME ....

ADDRESS ....

....

.... PHONE

.... FAX

I HAD THREE CHAIRS IN MY HOUSE: ONE FOR SOLITUDE, TWO FOR FRIENDSHIP, THREE FOR SOCIETY.

Henry David Thoreau

ONE DAY IN THE COUNTRY
IS WORTH A MONTH IN TOWN.

Christina Rossetti

NAME

ADDRESS

.... PHONE

.... FAX

NAME

ADDRESS

.... PHONE

.... FAX

NAME

ADDRESS

.... PHONE

.... FAX

NAME

ADDRESS

.... PHONE

.... FAX

NAME

ADDRESS

PHONE

FAX

NAME

ADDRESS

PHONE

FAX

NAME

ADDRESS

PHONE

FAX

NAME

ADDRESS

PHONE

FAX

NAME ....

ADDRESS ....

....

.... PHONE

.... FAX

NAME ....

ADDRESS ....

....

.... PHONE

.... FAX

NAME ....

ADDRESS ....

....

.... PHONE

.... FAX

NAME ....

ADDRESS ....

....

.... PHONE

.... FAX

NAME

ADDRESS

.... PHONE

.... FAX

NAME

ADDRESS

.... PHONE

.... FAX

NAME

ADDRESS

.... PHONE

.... FAX

NAME

ADDRESS

.... PHONE

.... FAX

NAME

ADDRESS

PHONE

FAX

NAME

ADDRESS

PHONE

FAX

NAME

ADDRESS

PHONE

FAX

NAME

ADDRESS

PHONE

FAX

NAME

ADDRESS

.... PHONE

.... FAX

NAME

ADDRESS

.... PHONE

.... FAX

NAME

ADDRESS

.... PHONE

.... FAX

NAME

ADDRESS

.... PHONE

.... FAX

EARTH LAUGHS IN FLOWERS.

Ralph Waldo Emerson

OLD SHOES AND OLD
FRIENDS ARE BEST.

**New England
Proverb**

NAME

ADDRESS

PHONE

FAX

NAME

ADDRESS

PHONE

FAX

NAME

ADDRESS

PHONE

FAX

NAME

ADDRESS

PHONE

FAX

NAME

ADDRESS

PHONE

FAX

NAME

ADDRESS

PHONE

FAX

NAME

ADDRESS

PHONE

FAX

NAME

ADDRESS

PHONE

FAX

NAME

ADDRESS

.... PHONE

.... FAX

NAME

ADDRESS

.... PHONE

.... FAX

NAME

ADDRESS

.... PHONE

.... FAX

NAME

ADDRESS

.... PHONE

.... FAX

NAME ....

ADDRESS ....

....

.... PHONE

.... FAX

NAME ....

ADDRESS ....

....

.... PHONE

.... FAX

NAME ....

ADDRESS ....

....

.... PHONE

.... FAX

NAME ....

ADDRESS ....

....

.... PHONE

.... FAX

NAME

ADDRESS

                                                    PHONE

                                                    FAX

NAME

ADDRESS

                                                    PHONE

                                                    FAX

NAME

ADDRESS

                                                    PHONE

                                                    FAX

NAME

ADDRESS

                                                    PHONE

                                                    FAX

F

NAME

ADDRESS

PHONE

FAX

NAME

ADDRESS

PHONE

FAX

NAME

ADDRESS

PHONE

FAX

NAME

ADDRESS

PHONE

FAX

THE BEST WAY TO
GET REAL ENJOYMENT
OUT OF THE GARDEN
IS TO PUT ON A
WIDE STRAW HAT,
DRESS IN THIN
LOOSE-FITTING
CLOTHES, HOLD A
LITTLE TROWEL IN
ONE HAND AND A
COOL DRINK IN THE
OTHER, AND TELL
THE MAN
WHERE TO DIG.

Charles Barr

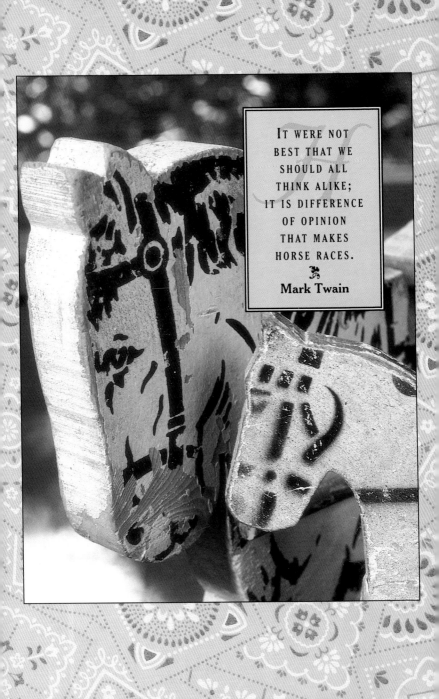

IT WERE NOT
BEST THAT WE
SHOULD ALL
THINK ALIKE;
IT IS DIFFERENCE
OF OPINION
THAT MAKES
HORSE RACES.

Mark Twain

NAME

ADDRESS

.... PHONE

.... FAX

NAME

ADDRESS

.... PHONE

.... FAX

NAME

ADDRESS

.... PHONE

.... FAX

NAME

ADDRESS

.... PHONE

.... FAX

G

NAME

ADDRESS

PHONE

FAX

NAME

ADDRESS

PHONE

FAX

NAME

ADDRESS

PHONE

FAX

NAME

ADDRESS

PHONE

FAX

NAME ....

ADDRESS ....

....

....PHONE

....FAX

NAME ....

ADDRESS ....

....

....PHONE

....FAX

NAME ....

ADDRESS ....

....

....PHONE

....FAX

NAME ....

ADDRESS ....

....

....PHONE

....FAX

NAME ....

ADDRESS ....

....

.... PHONE

.... FAX

....

NAME ....

ADDRESS ....

....

.... PHONE

.... FAX

....

NAME ....

ADDRESS ....

....

.... PHONE

.... FAX

....

NAME ....

ADDRESS ....

....

.... PHONE

.... FAX

....

NAME

ADDRESS

.... PHONE

.... FAX

NAME

ADDRESS

.... PHONE

.... FAX

NAME

ADDRESS

.... PHONE

.... FAX

NAME

ADDRESS

.... PHONE

.... FAX

NAME

ADDRESS

PHONE

FAX

NAME

ADDRESS

PHONE

FAX

NAME

ADDRESS

PHONE

FAX

NAME

ADDRESS

PHONE

FAX

IT IS ONLY WITH THE HEART THAT
ONE CAN SEE RIGHTLY;
WHAT IS ESSENTIAL IS INVISIBLE
TO THE EYE.

Antoine de Saint-Exupéry

A THING OF BEAUTY
IS A JOY FOREVER.

John Keats

I

NAME

ADDRESS

....

....PHONE

....FAX

NAME

ADDRESS

....

....PHONE

....FAX

NAME

ADDRESS

....

....PHONE

....FAX

NAME

ADDRESS

....

....PHONE

....FAX

I

NAME

ADDRESS

PHONE

FAX

NAME

ADDRESS

PHONE

FAX

NAME

ADDRESS

PHONE

FAX

NAME

ADDRESS

PHONE

FAX

I

NAME

ADDRESS

PHONE

FAX

NAME

ADDRESS

PHONE

FAX

NAME

ADDRESS

PHONE

FAX

NAME

ADDRESS

PHONE

FAX

NAME

ADDRESS

.... PHONE

.... FAX

NAME

ADDRESS

.... PHONE

.... FAX

NAME

ADDRESS

.... PHONE

.... FAX

NAME

ADDRESS

.... PHONE

.... FAX

NAME

ADDRESS

PHONE

FAX

NAME

ADDRESS

PHONE

FAX

NAME

ADDRESS

PHONE

FAX

NAME

ADDRESS

PHONE

FAX

NAME

ADDRESS

PHONE

FAX

NAME

ADDRESS

PHONE

FAX

NAME

ADDRESS

PHONE

FAX

NAME

ADDRESS

PHONE

FAX

KISSING DON'T LAST: COOKERY DO!

George Meredith

Lo, life again knocked laughing at the door!

Robert Browning

NAME

ADDRESS

.... PHONE

.... FAX

NAME

ADDRESS

.... PHONE

.... FAX

NAME

ADDRESS

.... PHONE

.... FAX

NAME

ADDRESS

.... PHONE

.... FAX

NAME ....

ADDRESS ....

....

.... PHONE

.... FAX

NAME ....

ADDRESS ....

....

.... PHONE

.... FAX

NAME ....

ADDRESS ....

....

.... PHONE

.... FAX

NAME ....

ADDRESS ....

....

.... PHONE

.... FAX

NAME

ADDRESS

.... PHONE

.... FAX

NAME

ADDRESS

.... PHONE

.... FAX

NAME

ADDRESS

.... PHONE

.... FAX

NAME

ADDRESS

.... PHONE

.... FAX

NAME

ADDRESS

....PHONE

....FAX

NAME

ADDRESS

....PHONE

....FAX

NAME

ADDRESS

....PHONE

....FAX

NAME

ADDRESS

....PHONE

....FAX

NAME

ADDRESS

.... PHONE

.... FAX

NAME

ADDRESS

.... PHONE

.... FAX

NAME

ADDRESS

.... PHONE

.... FAX

NAME

ADDRESS

.... PHONE

.... FAX

NAME ....

ADDRESS ....

....

.... PHONE

.... FAX

....

NAME ....

ADDRESS ....

....

.... PHONE

.... FAX

....

NAME ....

ADDRESS ....

....

.... PHONE

.... FAX

....

NAME ....

ADDRESS ....

....

.... PHONE

.... FAX

> YOUR FRIEND IS THE
> MAN WHO KNOWS ALL
> ABOUT YOU AND
> STILL LIKES YOU.
>
> **Henry David
> Thoreau**

TOMATOE

. . . 'GOOD FENCES
MAKE GOOD NEIGHBORS'.

Robert Frost

NAME

ADDRESS

.... PHONE

.... FAX

NAME

ADDRESS

.... PHONE

.... FAX

NAME

ADDRESS

.... PHONE

.... FAX

NAME

ADDRESS

.... PHONE

.... FAX

NAME ....

ADDRESS ....

....

.... PHONE

.... FAX

....

NAME ....

ADDRESS ....

....

.... PHONE

.... FAX

....

NAME ....

ADDRESS ....

....

.... PHONE

.... FAX

....

NAME ....

ADDRESS ....

....

.... PHONE

.... FAX

NAME

ADDRESS

....PHONE

....FAX

NAME

ADDRESS

....PHONE

....FAX

NAME

ADDRESS

....PHONE

....FAX

NAME

ADDRESS

....PHONE

....FAX

NAME ....

ADDRESS ....

....

.... PHONE

.... FAX

NAME ....

ADDRESS ....

....

.... PHONE

.... FAX

NAME ....

ADDRESS ....

....

.... PHONE

.... FAX

NAME ....

ADDRESS ....

....

.... PHONE

.... FAX

NAME

ADDRESS

.... PHONE

.... FAX

NAME

ADDRESS

.... PHONE

.... FAX

NAME

ADDRESS

.... PHONE

.... FAX

NAME

ADDRESS

.... PHONE

.... FAX

NAME

ADDRESS

PHONE

FAX

NAME

ADDRESS

PHONE

FAX

NAME

ADDRESS

PHONE

FAX

NAME

ADDRESS

PHONE

FAX

THE ORNAMENT
OF A HOUSE IS
THE FRIENDS WHO
FREQUENT IT.

**Ralph Waldo
Emerson**

'WILL YOU WALK INTO MY PARLOUR?'
SAID A SPIDER TO A FLY;
'TIS THE PRETTIEST LITTLE PARLOUR
THAT EVER YOU DID SPY.'

Mary Howitt

NAME

ADDRESS

PHONE

FAX

NAME

ADDRESS

PHONE

FAX

NAME

ADDRESS

PHONE

FAX

NAME

ADDRESS

PHONE

FAX

O

NAME

ADDRESS

PHONE

FAX

NAME

ADDRESS

PHONE

FAX

NAME

ADDRESS

PHONE

FAX

NAME

ADDRESS

PHONE

FAX

NAME

ADDRESS

....PHONE

....FAX

NAME

ADDRESS

....PHONE

....FAX

NAME

ADDRESS

....PHONE

....FAX

NAME

ADDRESS

....PHONE

....FAX

NAME ....

ADDRESS ....

....

.... PHONE

.... FAX

....

NAME ....

ADDRESS ....

....

.... PHONE

.... FAX

....

NAME ....

ADDRESS ....

....

.... PHONE

.... FAX

....

NAME ....

ADDRESS ....

....

.... PHONE

.... FAX

NAME

ADDRESS

....PHONE

....FAX

NAME

ADDRESS

....PHONE

....FAX

NAME

ADDRESS

....PHONE

....FAX

NAME

ADDRESS

....PHONE

....FAX

P

NAME ....

ADDRESS ....

....

.... PHONE

.... FAX

....

NAME ....

ADDRESS ....

....

.... PHONE

.... FAX

....

NAME ....

ADDRESS ....

....

.... PHONE

.... FAX

....

NAME ....

ADDRESS ....

....

.... PHONE

.... FAX

NO QUESTION
IS EVER SETTLED
UNTIL IT IS
SETTLED RIGHT.

**Ella Wheeler
Wilcox**

LET YOUR REST BE PERFECT
IN ITS SEASON, LIKE THE REST
OF WATERS THAT ARE STILL.

Philip G. Hamerton

NAME

ADDRESS

PHONE

FAX

NAME

ADDRESS

PHONE

FAX

NAME

ADDRESS

PHONE

FAX

NAME

ADDRESS

PHONE

FAX

NAME

ADDRESS

PHONE

FAX

NAME

ADDRESS

PHONE

FAX

NAME

ADDRESS

PHONE

FAX

NAME

ADDRESS

PHONE

FAX

NAME

ADDRESS

.... PHONE

.... FAX

NAME

ADDRESS

.... PHONE

.... FAX

NAME

ADDRESS

.... PHONE

.... FAX

NAME

ADDRESS

.... PHONE

.... FAX

NAME

ADDRESS

.... PHONE

.... FAX

NAME

ADDRESS

.... PHONE

.... FAX

NAME

ADDRESS

.... PHONE

.... FAX

NAME

ADDRESS

.... PHONE

.... FAX

NAME

ADDRESS

PHONE

FAX

NAME

ADDRESS

PHONE

FAX

NAME

ADDRESS

PHONE

FAX

NAME

ADDRESS

PHONE

FAX

R

NAME

ADDRESS

....

PHONE

FAX

NAME

ADDRESS

....

PHONE

FAX

NAME

ADDRESS

....

PHONE

FAX

NAME

ADDRESS

....

PHONE

FAX

AND THE SONG, FROM BEGINNING TO END,
I FOUND AGAIN IN THE HEART OF A FRIEND.

Henry Wadsworth Longfellow

LOVE AND SCANDAL
ARE THE
BEST SWEETENERS
OF TEA.

Anonymous

NAME

ADDRESS

PHONE

FAX

NAME

ADDRESS

PHONE

FAX

NAME

ADDRESS

PHONE

FAX

NAME

ADDRESS

PHONE

FAX

NAME ....

ADDRESS ....

....

.... PHONE

.... FAX

....

NAME ....

ADDRESS ....

....

.... PHONE

.... FAX

....

NAME ....

ADDRESS ....

....

.... PHONE

.... FAX

....

NAME ....

ADDRESS ....

....

.... PHONE

.... FAX

NAME

ADDRESS

.... PHONE

FAX

NAME

ADDRESS

.... PHONE

FAX

NAME

ADDRESS

.... PHONE

FAX

NAME

ADDRESS

.... PHONE

FAX

NAME ....

ADDRESS ....

....

.... PHONE

.... FAX

NAME ....

ADDRESS ....

....

.... PHONE

.... FAX

NAME ....

ADDRESS ....

....

.... PHONE

.... FAX

NAME ....

ADDRESS ....

....

.... PHONE

.... FAX

NAME

ADDRESS

PHONE

FAX

NAME

ADDRESS

PHONE

FAX

NAME

ADDRESS

PHONE

FAX

NAME

ADDRESS

PHONE

FAX

NAME ....

ADDRESS ....

....

.... PHONE

.... FAX

NAME ....

ADDRESS ....

....

.... PHONE

.... FAX

NAME ....

ADDRESS ....

....

.... PHONE

.... FAX

NAME ....

ADDRESS ....

....

.... PHONE

.... FAX

GOOSEY GOOSEY GANDER,
WHITHER SHALL
I WANDER?
UPSTAIRS AND
DOWNSTAIRS
AND IN MY LADY'S
CHAMBER.

THERE I MET AN OLD MAN
WHO WOULD NOT SAY
HIS PRAYERS.
I TOOK HIM BY THE
LEFT LEG,
AND KICKED HIM DOWN
THE STAIRS.

Nursery Rhyme

FRIENDSHIP INCREASES BY VISITING
FRIENDS, BUT BY VISITING SELDOM.

Benjamin Franklin

NAME

ADDRESS

PHONE

FAX

NAME

ADDRESS

PHONE

FAX

NAME

ADDRESS

PHONE

FAX

NAME

ADDRESS

PHONE

FAX

NAME

ADDRESS

                                            PHONE
                                            FAX

NAME

ADDRESS

                                            PHONE
                                            FAX

NAME

ADDRESS

                                            PHONE
                                            FAX

NAME

ADDRESS

                                            PHONE
                                            FAX

NAME

ADDRESS

....PHONE

....FAX

NAME

ADDRESS

....PHONE

....FAX

NAME

ADDRESS

....PHONE

....FAX

NAME

ADDRESS

....PHONE

....FAX

NAME

ADDRESS

.... PHONE

.... FAX

NAME

ADDRESS

.... PHONE

.... FAX

NAME

ADDRESS

.... PHONE

.... FAX

NAME

ADDRESS

.... PHONE

.... FAX

NAME

ADDRESS

PHONE

FAX

NAME

ADDRESS

PHONE

FAX

NAME

ADDRESS

PHONE

FAX

NAME

ADDRESS

PHONE

FAX

NAME
ADDRESS

.... PHONE
.... FAX

NAME
ADDRESS

.... PHONE
.... FAX

NAME
ADDRESS

.... PHONE
.... FAX

NAME
ADDRESS

.... PHONE
.... FAX

THERE IS NOTHING MORE SATISFYING THAN TO LIE
IN BED AT NIGHT, SECURE AND WARM, WITH A
WHISTLING WIND OUTSIDE.

Clare Leighton

MEN EXPECT TOO
MUCH, DO TOO LITTLE.
Allen Tate

NAME

ADDRESS

PHONE

FAX

NAME

ADDRESS

PHONE

FAX

NAME

ADDRESS

PHONE

FAX

NAME

ADDRESS

PHONE

FAX

NAME

ADDRESS

....PHONE

....FAX

NAME

ADDRESS

....PHONE

....FAX

NAME

ADDRESS

....PHONE

....FAX

NAME

ADDRESS

....PHONE

....FAX

NAME

ADDRESS

.... PHONE

.... FAX

NAME

ADDRESS

.... PHONE

.... FAX

NAME

ADDRESS

.... PHONE

.... FAX

NAME

ADDRESS

.... PHONE

.... FAX

X

NAME

ADDRESS

PHONE

FAX

NAME

ADDRESS

PHONE

FAX

NAME

ADDRESS

PHONE

FAX

NAME

ADDRESS

PHONE

FAX

NAME

ADDRESS

PHONE

FAX

NAME

ADDRESS

PHONE

FAX

NAME

ADDRESS

PHONE

FAX

NAME

ADDRESS

PHONE

FAX

NAME

ADDRESS

PHONE

FAX

NAME

ADDRESS

PHONE

FAX

NAME

ADDRESS

PHONE

FAX

NAME

ADDRESS

PHONE

FAX

YOU ARE AS
WELCOME AS
THE FLOWERS
IN MAY.

**Charles
Macklin**

ZIP-A-DEE-DOO-DAH
ZIP-A-DEE-AY
MY, OH MY,
    WHAT A WONDERFUL DAY!

**Allie Wrubel and
Ray Gilbert**

NAME

ADDRESS

....

.... PHONE

.... FAX

NAME

ADDRESS

....

.... PHONE

.... FAX

NAME

ADDRESS

....

.... PHONE

.... FAX

NAME

ADDRESS

....

.... PHONE

.... FAX

NAME

ADDRESS

.... PHONE

.... FAX

NAME

ADDRESS

.... PHONE

.... FAX

NAME

ADDRESS

.... PHONE

.... FAX

NAME

ADDRESS

.... PHONE

.... FAX

NAME

ADDRESS

PHONE

FAX

NAME

ADDRESS

PHONE

FAX

NAME

ADDRESS

PHONE

FAX

NAME

ADDRESS

PHONE

FAX

NAME ....

ADDRESS ....

....

.... PHONE

.... FAX

NAME ....

ADDRESS ....

....

.... PHONE

.... FAX

NAME ....

ADDRESS ....

....

.... PHONE

.... FAX

NAME ....

ADDRESS ....

....

.... PHONE

.... FAX

NAME

ADDRESS

PHONE

FAX

NAME

ADDRESS

PHONE

FAX

NAME

ADDRESS

PHONE

FAX

NAME

ADDRESS

PHONE

FAX

NAME

ADDRESS

PHONE

FAX

NAME

ADDRESS

PHONE

FAX

NAME

ADDRESS

PHONE

FAX

NAME

ADDRESS

PHONE

FAX

BIRTHDAYS

Name...

Date ....

Name...

Date ....

Name...

Date ....

Name...

Date ....

Name...

Date ....

Name...

Date ....

Name...

Date ....

Name ....

Date ....

Name ....

Date ....

Name ....

Date ....

Name ....

Date ....

Name ....

Date ....

Name ....

Date ....

Name ....

Date ....

Name...

Date ....

Name...

Date ....

Name...

Date ....

Name...

Date ....

Name...

Date ....

Name...

Date ....

Name...

Date ....

ANNIVERSARIES

Name...

Date ....

Name...

Date ....

Name...

Date ....

Name...

Date ....

Name...

Date ....

Name...

Date ....

Name...

Date ....

Name..

Date ....

Name..

Date ....

Name..

Date ....

Name..

Date ....

Name..

Date ....

Name..

Date ....

Name..

Date ....

Name ....

Date ....

Name ....

Date ....

Name ....

Date ....

Name ....

Date ....

Name ....

Date ....

Name ....

Date ....

Name ....

Date ....

ANNIVERSARY GIFTS

First . . . . Paper
Second . . . . Cotton
Third . . . . Leather
Fourth . . . . Books
Fifth . . . . . . Wood or Clocks
Tenth . . . . Tin or Aluminum
Fifteenth . . . . Crystal
Twentieth . . . . China

Twenty-fifth . . . . Silver
Thirtieth . . . . Pearl
Thirty-fifth . . . . Coral or Jade
Fortieth . . . . Ruby
Forty-fifth . . . . Sapphire
Fiftieth . . . . Gold
Fifty-fifth . . . . Emerald
Sixtieth . . . . Diamond

BIRTHSTONES

January . . . . Garnet
February . . . . Amethyst
March . . . . Aquamarine
April . . . . Diamond
May . . . . Emerald
June . . . . Pearl
July . . . . Ruby
August . . . . Peridot
September . . . . Sapphire
October . . . . Opal
November . . . . Topaz
December . . . . Turquoise

TOWNFOLK KNOW
PLEASURES,
COUNTRY PEOPLE JOYS.

Minna
Thomas
Antrim

IMPORTANT PHONE NUMBERS

Police Department ....

Fire Department ....

Doctor ....

Hospital ....

Poison Control Center ....

School ....

Plumber ....

Electrician ....

Heat/Air Conditioning ....

Mechanic ....

Other ....

Credits and Acknowledgments

Front Cover Photograph by Keith Scott Morton.

A, B (Front) Photograph by Keith Scott Morton; excerpt from "Mr. Gilfil's Love Story," in *Scenes of Clerical Life* by George Eliot. (Back) Photograph by Keith Scott Morton; excerpt from *Alice in Wonderland* by Lewis Carroll.

C, D (Front) Photograph by Jessie Walker; excerpt from "Visitors," in *Walden* by Henry David Thoreau. (Back) Photograph by Keith Scott Morton; excerpt from "Summer" by Christina Rossetti.

E, F (Front) Photograph by Peter Vital; excerpt from "Hamatreya," in *Poems* by Ralph Waldo Emerson. (Back) Photograph by Keith Scott Morton; excerpt from a New England proverb.

G, H (Front) Photograph by Doug Kennedy; excerpt from Charles Barr, quoted in *The New York Times*, July 11, 1948. (Back) Photograph by Jessie Walker; excerpt from *Pudd'nhead Wilson* by Mark Twain.

I, J (Front) Photograph by Keith Scott Morton; excerpt from *The Little Prince* by Antoine de Saint-Exupéry. (Back) Photograph by Keith Scott Morton; excerpt from *Endymion* by John Keats.

K, L (Front) Photograph by Paul Kopelow; excerpt from *The Ordeal of Richard Feverel* by George Meredith. (Back) Photograph by Keith Scott Morton; excerpt from *Balaustion's Adventure* by Robert Browning.

M, N (Front) Photograph by Keith Scott Morton; excerpt from Henry David Thoreau. (Back) Photograph by Keith Scott Morton; excerpt from "Mending a Wall" by Robert Frost.

O, P (Front) Photograph by Keith Scott Morton; excerpt from "Domestic Life," in *Society and Solitude* by Ralph Waldo Emerson. (Back) Photograph by Feliciano; excerpt from "The Spider and the Fly" by Mary Howitt.

Q, R (Front) Photograph by Keith Scott Morton; excerpt from "Settle the Question Right" by Ella Wheeler Wilcox. (Back) Photograph by Michael Dunne; excerpt from *The Intellectual Life* by Philip G. Hamerton.

S, T (Front) Photograph by Jessie Walker; excerpt from "The Arrow and the Song" by Henry Wadsworth Longfellow. (Back) Photograph by Paul Kopelow; excerpt from *The Ordeal of Richard Feverel* by George Meredith.

U, V (Front) Photograph by Keith Scott Morton; excerpt from a traditional nursery rhyme. (Back) Photograph by Doug Kennedy; excerpt from *Poor Richard's Almanack* by Benjamin Franklin.

W, X (Front) Photograph by Al Teufen; excerpt from *Four Hedges* by Claire Leighton. (Back) Photograph by Keith Scott Morton; excerpt from "To the Lacedemonians" by Allen Tate.

Y, Z (Front) Photograph by Paul Kopelow; excerpt from Charles Macklin. (Back) Photograph by Paul Kopelow; excerpt from "Zip-A-Dee-Doo-Dah" by Allie Wrubel and Ray Gilbert.

Birthdays and Anniversaries (Front) Photograph by Richard Jeffery. (Back) Photograph by Paul Kopelow.

Back Cover (Left) Photograph by Keith Scott Morton. (Right) Photograph by Jessie Walker.

It is the policy of William Morrow and Company, Inc.,
and its imprints and affiliates, recognizing the importance of preserving
what has been written, to print the books we publish on acid-free paper,
and we exert our best efforts to that end.

ISBN: 0-688-13409-2

Printed in Singapore
First Edition
1 2 3 4 5 6 7 8 9 10

For Country Living
Rachel Newman, Editor-in-Chief
Niña Williams, Executive Editor
Julio Vega, Art Director
Mary R. Roby, Managing Editor
John Mack Carter, Director, Magazine Development

Produced by Smallwood and Stewart, Inc., New York City

Edited by Rachel Carley
Designed by Jan Melchior

Notice: Every effort has been made to locate the copyright owners of
the material used in this book. Please let us know if an error has been made,
and we will make any necessary changes in subsequent printings.